Love It!

234 Inspirations and Activities
to Help You Love Your Body

By Ragen Chastain, Jeanette DePatie & Pia Schiavo-Campo

Illustrated by Toni Tails

Real Big Publishing

Love It ! 234 Inspirations and Activities to Help You Love Your Body

Copyright © 2016 by Ragen Chastain and Jeanette DePatie.

For information contact :

Real Big Publishing : 710 S. Myrtle Ave. #233, Monrovia, CA 91016

http://www.realbigpublishing.com/

Cover design by Toni Tails

ISBN: 978-0-9833437-2-1

First Edition: December 2016

10 9 8 7 6 5 4 3 2 1

CONTENTS

Foreword

HOW TO USE THIS BOOK

WE DECIDED TO PUT THIS BOOK TOGETHER because it is the kind of resource that we'd like to have and we hope that you enjoy using the book as much as we've enjoyed writing it. Before you get started, we wanted to give you some thoughts about using the book that we think might be helpful.

It's in no particular order. You can start at the beginning and go to the end. You can open it up to a random page. You can read through until an activity strikes you. We recommend that you consider keeping a journal (maybe even a blog) about your experiences during these body love sessions so you can remember what you learned. You can even repeat experiences and watch how you've grown and changed.

Not all of these activities may work for you as written, and that's one of the reasons we've included over 200 activities.

When you come across an experience that doesn't work for you, for whatever reason, you can choose to skip it or modify it to work for you. Remember that this is your journey and this book is created to support you – not to limit you. Feel free to choose your own adventure and modify to make this work best for you. We've also included calendars and notes pages in the book to help you shape your journey and track your progress.

Finally, we recommend that you think of this as an experiment and approach it with curiosity. If you find that you are stuck with an exercise, or experiencing a lot of discomfort, remember that you can choose to push through, or you can decide this isn't the right thing for you to be doing right now and try something else.

Your relationship with your body will last a lifetime, so take your time and find joy in the journey.

Yours in Body Love,
Ragen, Jeanette & Pia

The Tips

Choose to wear something that feels super comfortable. Pay attention to really feeling good in your body in comfy clothes.

***

Write a letter to your younger self. Tell that younger version what things about them you are grateful for, are proud of, and appreciate. Then tell them what you wish you had known at that age.

***

Buy a full-length mirror. Spend 5 minutes looking into it and giving yourself compliments. If the compliments don't come quickly, that's ok. You can start by just looking in the mirror and working on feeling neutral. Or just think of one compliment and keep repeating it until another one comes to mind. Do this exercise each day until it becomes easy. Then use it as a pick-me-up whenever you need it.

***

Wear your cutest pair of shoes to show off your amazing feet.

***

Sit in front of a roaring fire. Feel and appreciate each part of your body as it warms up.

***

The Day Can Change in an Instant

Several patients have shared with me various permutations of the same story to which you can perhaps relate: One moment they are having a great day in a way that either celebrates their bodies (such as dancing, wearing a beautiful dress or going for a hikc) or seemingly has little to do with their size, shape or appearance at all (such as sharing a meal with a friend, enjoying a great book, or being productive at the home or office.)

Then it happens: a glance in a mirror, a reflection in a car window, a lover's comment, a stranger's glare or a similar trigger creates a cascade of negative feelings about their bodies. Toward the bottom of the spiral is the temptation to change their size or shape. The day is ruined. Or is it?

My patients find that a simple but often effective remedy is to remember that the body they are currently so down on is the same one they had earlier in the day when they were feeling great. In other words, they know from recent firsthand experience that they do not actually need to change their size or shape to enjoy life and feel good about themselves, that they are capable of those things in their bodies just as they are. Sometimes this quick reminder is all they need.

If this happens to you, remember, the day can change in an instant. So change it back.

--Jonah Soolman

http://www.soolmannutrition.com/

Go to a dance club and shake your groove thing. Focus on having fun and feeling good while moving your body to the music.

***

Participate in a boudoir photo shoot. Put the pictures in a photo book. Flip through them once a day for a week (or more) and find at least one thing you like in every picture.

***

Sing a body positive song out loud or in your head as you move through your day.

Protest something body negative. Whether it's sending an e-mail to a company who airs commercials designed to take your self-esteem and sell it back at a profit, or to a fashion magazine that doesn't show enough bodies like yours, search online sites for petitions to support. Your body is awesome. Give it your full-throated support.

***

Find and read a new body-positive blog. Consider one that is written by someone with multiple marginalized identies—a Person of Color, Queer, Trans, Gender Non-Binary, Disabled Person or Person with Disabilities.

***

Take a class that engages your body—dance, painting, fitness, gardening or whatever strikes your fancy. Stay in gratitude and joy for your amazing body and its ability to do stuff.

***

Spend a day noticing when you compare your body with other people's bodies. Each time you notice, say to yourself, "All bodies are good bodies—INCLUDING MINE!"

***

Choose to experience a "guilt-free" holiday or feast. Taste all the flavor in every single bite, and enjoyall the food you want without any guilt or remorse.

***

Dress up like a body positive hero you admire—whether it's for Halloween, cos-play, a con, or just because you feel like it.

***

Find some items of clothing that haven't fit for a year or more. Give them away to charity or have a clothing swap with some friends.

***

Get yourself a fabulous accessory—a hat, a feather boa, a ring, or whatever. Your body is awesome, so adorn it!

***

Get a health test that you've boon putting off. Be conscious that this is a way that you take care of your body.

***

Create a body love meetup with your friends or in your community.

***

Spend some time with the earth, getting your hands dirty in the garden, sitting under a tree, having a picnic outside, hiking, swimming, just sitting in a room with a beautiful view, or surfing beautiful nature pictures on your computer, and think about how your body is part of the natural beauty that is all around us.

Color in the picture below. Use the color key below to determine which colors to use. The color should coordinate with how you feel about each of the body parts depicted below.

Color Key
Blue=gorgeous, purple=luscious, red=sexy, black=strong, green=beautiful, yellow=dazzling, orange=hot, pink=pretty.

Enjoy getting (or giving yourself) a facial or a face and head massage. Your face and head do a lot for you. Now you're doing something for them.

*****

Shut off the alarm clock, draw the shades and sleep as late as your body wants to. Luxuriate in how good it feels to be well rested.

*****

Make a playlist on your computer or phone or MP3 player that is a "soundtrack" for your body—full of songs that make you feel awesome, songs that remind you to appreciate your body, and songs that remind you that the haters don't matter.

*****

Get a deal on a great hotel and pamper your body for a weekend. Realize that your body is totally worth all this extra care.

*****

Wear something that shows some skin—tummy, shoulders, legs—you pick! Be proud of your awesome body!

***

Splurge on your favorite foods. Focus on how much you are enjoying each morsel of food, and than your body for the ability to taste all that deliciousness.

Dance Naked Like Everybody's Watching

I love to dance and I love to be naked. The former has always been true, the latter not so much. I spent many years letting my body shame dictate every aspect of my life—from what I ate, to what I wore, to how I moved. But when I was dancing, I almost felt free...almost. I knew that making peace with my body was the key to being truly free, whether I was dancing or not. So I got naked. I got real naked, and I got real naked as often as possible. I looked at myself naked. I swam naked. I slept naked. I wrote naked. I cooked naked – NOT something I recommend, but you get the idea. My house was dubbed the "naked house" by a few neighbors who happened to look in my windows at opportune times. (And I would like to state for the record that there were no complaints.) I have no idea what I looked like the first time I danced naked down my stairs, singing along to Linda Eder's "Big Time", but I felt magical, and that my friends, is all that matters.

So get naked, and get dancing to any song that makes you want to shake your ass. I have too many to even attempt to list, and I suspect you do too. On a final note, why dance like EVERYBODY is watching? As Harry Winston said, "People will stare. Make it worth their while."

--Courtney Joy Hanneman

http://www.functionalgirl.com/

***

Buy a sex toy that seems like it would be really fun to try! Think about how awesome your body's ability to feel pleasure is.

***

Spend some time searching online for pictures of people who look like you, save them, and create a slide show. Watch it every day for 30 days, and find something beautiful about each person in every slide.

***

See a healthcare practitioner and get your moles checked out. Feel really proud of the good care you are taking of your body.

***

Get some friends together for a Body Positive Party! Have some delicious food, and compliment each other. Do some of the exercises from this book, give each other mani/pedis—whatever helps you all appreciate your body more.

***

Think of a time your body let you down. Forgive your body and thank it for everything it does for you.

Take a picture of yourself in a swimsuit. Write compliments all over the picture in permanent marker and then tape the picture to your mirror, computer, refrigerator or some other place that you see every day.

Plant something. Enjoy the feeling of getting your hands dirty and think about how cool it is that your body can help bring something else to life.

***

Make art with your own body. Have a photo shoot or use an online service turn a photograph of you into an oil painting. Hang the art somewhere you can appreciate it a lot.

***

Speak out against Photoshop manipulation of images of people. Remind yourself that the pictures we're told to compare ourselves to don't even accurately represent the people in the pictures.

***

Stand up for your body when somebody says something negative about bodies like yours. Try saying something like, "All bodies are good bodies, and I'm sad for you that you don't know that.

***

Take a yoga class either in public or at home. Enjoy the feelings of stretch and strength and even struggle in your body.

Spend some time looking at family photos. Thank your family for giving you the traits you enjoy in your face and your body.

***

When someone makes a comment or gives advice about your body, health or choices that you didn't ask for, interrupt and tell them you are not soliciting outside opinions about your personal choices.

***

Have a "Dealing with Jerks" party. Get your friends together and write down all the things people say to you about your body, health, or choices that are inappropriate. Take turns coming up with responses and practicing them on each other.

***

Become conscious of your negative body thoughts. Choose one thought at a time and ask yourself, "Where did this idea come from? Did it come from someone who makes a profit if I believe it? Is this thought serving me? Am I ready to let it go?"

***

Do a "stone soup event" where you decide on a theme (tacos, soup, stew, etc.) and everyone brings an ingredient. Make it a positive body talk event with no weight loss talk or negative body talk allowed. Enjoy cooking and eating in a like-minded community.

***

Talk to someone in your life who says things that make you feel bad about your body. Let them know that it's not okay to say those things to you, and that in order for the relationship to continue, they will need to stop.

***

Join a meet-up, Facebook, or other group dedicated to body positivity.

***

Wear a body positive t-shirt. Walk around and realize that you are using your awesome body to let other people know they have options other than hating their bodies.

***

Try a new shade of lipstick, new cologne, perfume or aftershave. Enjoy how it feels going on your body. Think of it as a fun way to reward your body for everything it does for you.

***

Pick a piece of fruit that you feel echoes your body's shape. Carve a bikini or swimsuit into it (with the peel) and notice how adorable it is. Put a picture of your head on top for a little body positive art.

***

Go to bed an hour early and relax before bedtime so that your body can get some really good rest. As you drift off, thank your body for all the work it will be doing while you sleep.

***

Practice the Underpants Rule. I am the boss of my underpants. Everyone else is the boss of their underpants. There is no Underpants Overlord. When it comes to my body, I get to make choices for me and other people get to make choices for them.

***

Wear something in your favorite color. Let it help you feel extra confident and happy with your body as you move around the world.

***

Consciously do a mini-celebration every time you engage in a behavior that honors your body.

***

Look at yourself in a full-length mirror before you head out the door. Give yourself at least 2 compliments.

***

Make something wonderful to eat, from scratch, just for you. Enjoy the feelings of making it and eating it.

***

Snuggle up under a warm blanket. Feel the blanket against your skin. Notice the warmth and comfort and take this time to feel really good in your body.

***

Write a letter from an older version of you, telling you how awesome your life was because you learned to love your body just as it is each day.

***

Think of someone who gave you negative ideas about your body. Decide to forgive them, or to not let them affect how you feel about your body. (You don't have to tell them.)

***

Create a team for a charity walk / run / roll or other event. Create a training schedule and/or online chat group to talk about your training and have a "positive body talk only" rule.

***

Give appropriate body positive compliments to 5 people you see. Learn to see the same things in your own body.

***

Consider that perhaps we've been lied to about beauty – that in fact everyone is beautiful, and the ability to perceive it is a skillset that can be developed – so if someone can't see your beauty it's not because it isn't there, but because they haven't developed their skillset.

***

Curvy Loving-Kindness Meditation

Repeat to yourself as often as you'd like.

May I greet my body with gentleness.

May I soften when life invites me to harden.

May I listen to my intuition with wisdom and trust it with ease.

May I appreciate my body a little more in this moment, just as it is.

- Anna Guest -Jelley

www.curvyyoga.com/

Take selfies over a period of time (week, month, etc.,) go through them, and find something about your body to appreciate in each one.

***

Find a doctor you can trust and build a mutually respectful relationship.

Get a pair of shoes that fit perfectly. Your hardworking feet deserve good shoes. As you wear them, feel how they support your feet on this journey.

***

Each day for the next week, think of a specific body part—your hand, foot, thigh, stomach, etc, and think of all the things that body part does for you and express your deep appreciation.

***

Get a manicure, maybe with special designs and gems, or maybe with no polish and just buffing. Spend some time each day this week appreciating your hands and everything they do for you.

***

Look in a mirror and look deeply into your own eyes. Notice how beautiful and how unique your eyes are and appreciate what they can do.

***

Take action to make a public space more accommodating of body diversity. Think about how worthy your body is of being accommodated and how this space should have been accommodating in the first place.

***

Spend some time soaking up the sun. Take care of your body by putting on some sunscreen, feeling the warm rays on your body, thinking about the Vitamin D you're getting and thanking your body for being able to not only enjoy, but also use the power of the sun.

***

Help a child to appreciate their body. Compliment a kid that you know or compliment a kid in the store—maybe about how strong they are or how awesome their hair is. Take time to appreciate that same thing in your own body.

***

Subscribe to a blog that helps you love and appreciate your body.

***

Wear something that makes you feel fancy and special. Choose movie star sunglasses, a boa, a tiara or a great hat and ROCK it!

Before you get out of bed in the morning, gently stretch every muscle. Feel your body stretch and wake up.

***

Sled, bike, skateboard, run or roll down a hill. (How steep is totally up to you.) Feel the wind on your face. Notice how your body moves easily through space aided by gravity. Feel the exhilaration.

***

Write an email to an Oscar winning actress and tell her how much you love her work. Don't mention her red-carpet dress. Remind yourself that you can opt out of the belief that the only good body is a body that looks like the current stereotype of beauty, and realize that all bodies are good bodies.

***

Get a photo taken wearing no makeup or unshaved and spend some time appreciating yourself exactly how you wake up in the morning.

***

Paying Attention

In all my work with women we talk about Body Love Principles. We explore the most foundational principle to any type of change and that is AWARENESS—something so simple, and yet, so profound in its impact.

We need to start noticing our thoughts to begin changing them. Most of our issues that keep us stuck in body hatred or self-sabotage come from deep in our subconscious—formed from experiences in our younger years. Paying attention is the first step! This requires being present and not zoning out, or "going unconscious"—otherwise known as autopilot.

Today take a few moments to center yourself with some calming deep breathing, and when you are ready, in your journal reflect. What is your body saying to you? What does it want you to pay more attention to?

--Michelle Hess

http://bravegirl.me/

Get your teeth cleaned and then flash those pearly whites—knowing you are taking good care of your awesome mouth.

***

Write a thank you card to your body for all it does for you.

***

Spend a day noticing every time you have a negative thought about your body. Gently remind yourself that your body is wonderful right now as it is. At the end of the day, journal about what you've learned.

Help make your workplace more body positive. Put up a body-positive poster in your office or cubicle. Use a mug or put up a poster with a body positive message.

***

Imagine a fashion show runway is in your living room. Practice your runway walk and imagine everyone in the audience appreciating your amazing body.

***

Write a body positive slogan and post it on your blog or social media site.

***

Get a gentle foot massage. Spend some time in wonder of all the bones, mucles, tendons and ligaments in your feet and all the wonderful things that they do for you. Feel deep gratitude for them.

***

Spend time looking at photos on a body positive website. Notice the similarities between bodies on the site that you find attractive and your body.

The next time someone gives you a compliment, don't try to talk them out of it. Just say the magic words, "Thank you!" Then think to yourself, "What they said is totally true!"

***

Participate in a fitness event like a 5K or a fun run. Don't worry about how fast you're going. Just enjoy moving your body.

***

Treat your body to some relaxation. Sit on the porch or a park bench and enjoy a cup of coffee or tea. Pay attention to feeling grounded in your body as you relax.

***

Choose not to wear clothes that squeeze or "slim" you. Focus on loving your body's unique natural shape and letting it breathe.

***

Take everything that is too small for you out of your closet and box it up, sell it, or give it away.

Start a body love tree. Text, Facebook message, e-mail or write three friends with a compliment about how awesome their bodies are. Challenge them to accept the compliment, and then contact three friends and ask those three friends to do the same. Watch the body love increase exponentially.

***

Eat in front of a mirror. As you take each bite, feel how your body is amazing at getting energy from food and feel gratitude for the nourishment of your fabulous body.

***

Go spend some time playing with some kids. Notice how happy and free they are in their bodies and try to duplicate that with your own body.

***

Write a letter to somebody who has said something negative about your appearance. Let them know how they hurt you. You can send it, keep it, or burn it once you are done.

***

Have fantastic sex all by yourself.

***

Consider the concept of "flattering" as it's used to suggest that the only good clothing is the clothing that makes us look as thin as possible, covers our rolls and squeezes us into a particular shape. Consider opting out. Realize we can choose the clothes we wea for whatever reason we want (including that we just like them) and that we can opt out of "flattering" any time we want to.

Morning Glory

Encourages you to:

- Look at your body.
- Move your body (as little or as much as your body allows comfortably).
- Feel your body.

On mornings before you get dressed repeat (a minimum of 3 times) this mantra in your favorite melody. Don't be afraid to shake that birthday suit of yours, hands on your hips or waving in the air like you just don't care.

"I'm a big bright burning star and I'm gonna shine forever!"

If you are alone, take to the hills and belt it at the top of your lungs. If volume is an issue, a dedicated whisper or hum does the trick. If sound or movement isn't possible, internal repetition is equally effective. The power is in the words. I created this one many years ago, and even on mornings when I don't believe it, committing to doing it helps remind me that I should.

Author's Note: This activity can be adapted (with clothes on of course) for the workplace, public transit, school, banking or medical institutions and other other potentially traumatic public spaces. It cannot break down or protect you from systemic barriers or everyday body and race-based discrimination, but it has provided me a temporary space in the moment of violence to breathe through my pain, anger or frustration (as opposed to ignorant retaliation) so I can get back to regrouping my thoughts and planning my next steps for advocacy.

--Jill "Ji!!" Andrew, PhD(c.)

http://www.bodyconfidencecanadaawards.com/

Moisturize your entire body, head to toe. As you touch each part, appreciate each part.

***

Wear your hair in a fancy style—whether by styling your actual hair, using a wig or weave, or adding accessories—and appreciate how your hair can rock different looks.

***

When you hear an advertisement or message that makes you feel bad about your body, rewrite it (in your head, in your journal, etc.) into the body positive message it should be.

***

Pick an item of clothing you "like" and transform it into something that you "love"! Cut it, "Be-dazzle" it, take it to seamstress to have it altered, or do whatever it takes to make it perfect for you.

***

Do an event where you move your body for a charity—whether it's a charity walk/run/roll, or volunteering for a food pantry or doing a build for Habitat for Humanity. Feel gratitude for what your body can do to help others.

***

Figure out what food will nourish you in this moment. (Don't think too hard about it, just take the first thing that comes to mind.) Eat it, and enjoy every bite. Try listening to your body when it comes to what you eat. Google intuitive eating and see if it's something that you'd like to try.

***

Get a bunch of friends together and have a beauty pagent. Take turns crowning one another king/queen of different body-positive categories. Remember you get bonus points for being the queen/king of something truly funny or ridiculous!

Wear a body positive button.

***

Have a piece of clothing custom made for you.

***

Pick a theme song for your body. Play it lots. When you get sick of it, pick a new song.

***

Make a YouTube video talking about body love.

***

Fill in the blanks: I love my _____ because _____.

***

Get a massage.

***

Wear fabulous underwear.

***

Sing a love song to yourself.

***

Draw a loving self-portrait.

***

See a body-positive film or documentary.

***

Take your body on a trip to a spa.

***

Take your self-love journey one day at a time—or even one minute at a time, if that's what it takes. Give yourself permission to take your own path—however slow and winding that may be.

***

Make a pact with the friends you spend a lot of time with, not to engage in any negative body talk.

***

LOVE IT!

Do a meditation focused on body appreciation. You can write one for yourself, or find one online. For something simple, start at your toes and acknowledge each body part saying, "My [toes] are amazing. They help me [wear flipflops] they feel great [in the grass]. Thank you toes. I love and appreciate you." Move on to your feet, ankles, calves, etc and go all the way up your body. You can write it out at first, so that you don't have to think too hard about it as you go through the meditation. (Hint: if you're not fond of meditating, just write it out.)

***

Find art that features someone who looks like you. Display it where you'll see it often.

***

Write an email to a celebrity who looks like you. Tell them why they are a great role model for you.

***

My body is not the enemy. Repeat or write this down 20 times in the morning and 20 times at night.

***

Who are your role models?

Unfortunately, our mainstream media generally only shows thin, white, young role models in its depictions of "success" —i.e., playing the lead role in a film, being on the cover of a magazine, or otherwise enjoying "success" as it is portrayed to us by the media. Because we usually only see "success stories" depicted by thin women, many women correlate success with being a certain size — that is, we start to believe that success is only possible for thin women, simply because we don't see non-thin examples of "success" depicted.

Cultivating non-thin role models is an incredibly impactful way to combat the effects of thin-only media. When we see non-thin women doing all the things we hold ourselves back from on account of our weight, things like going on dates, wearing bikinis, or otherwise taking the world by storm, we start to believe that we can do those things too. Un-following media that contributes to our belief that thin equals success, and following positive media outlets that show us a new perspective, can dramatically influence our beliefs about what we're capable of in the bodies we have.

Who are you following on social media? What role models are you allowing into your sphere of influence? While we don't have full control over the media we consume, exerting control where we do have it is incredibly important, especially with the rise of social media.

--Isabel Foxen Duke

http://www.stopfightingfood.com/

Take a moment to imagine how you would feel about your body if its awesomeness were affirmed from the time you were a kid. What if every single negative thing everyone has ever told you about your body was a lie? How would your life be different? Consider deciding that this is exactly what happened and acting as if you would if you had known the truth about your body all along.

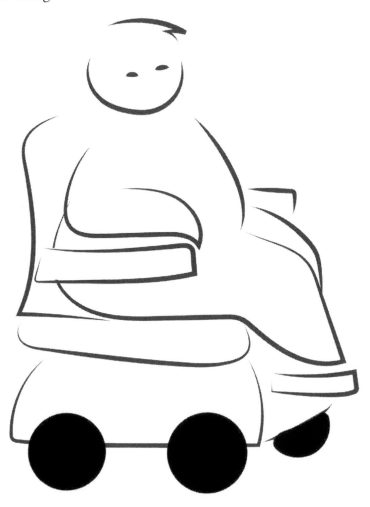

Grounding Meditation for Self-Connection

Finding self-love can be daunting. A good way to begin the journey is to find a simply way to connect with your body, appreciate what it does for you, and perhaps eventually get to accepting —even loving— it. Try this simple grounding meditation for self-connection. (Consider recording for easy listening.)

Lie comfortably on your back (pillows under knees/head are helpful).

Close your eyes. Start taking deeper breaths. Stay relaxed, no need to over-strive. Stay 5-10 breaths.

Place hands on belly, arms relaxed (tuck fingers into waistband if need be), and feel in to your breath as it moves under your hands. Expand, contract. Expand, contract. Stay 5-10 breaths.

Feel the way your back-body meets the ground. See if you can deepen this connection with each long exhale, letting yourself get heavy, one body area at a time. Stay 5-10 breaths.

If you feel so inclined, see if you can find something your body does that you appreciate and linger on that thought for 3 breaths. It can be something as simple as, "my eyes blink," or "my heart beats." Or try saying to yourself, "I accept myself," on 3 exhales.

If your mind wants to fight this, simply come back to feeling your breath under your hands and complete 3 breaths this way. Keep returning to your breath with every tug in another direction.

Gently open your eyes and return to natural breathing. Take a stretch through the length of your body and turn to your side. Stay on your side for 3 conscious breaths, note how you feel

-- Tiina Veer

http://www.tiinaveer.com/

CHASTAIN, DEPATIE, SCHIAVO-CAMPO

Wear some butt-hugging pants, and take some time to appreciate your rockin' booty!

***

Send a thank you note on behalf of your body to a merchant that is body positive.

***

Check the ergonomics of your workplace. Are your chair, desk, keyboard and monitor all in the correct position to keep you pain free? If not, fix it and notice how good it feels to make sure your body is properly supported.

***

Spend some time imagining a world without weight bias. What would it look like? How would it be different? How could you make some of these things a reality in your life right now? Make a plan for one of those things and start on it now.

***

Different is not bad, it's just different. You rock as you are!

***

Cancel your subscription to a fashion magazine. Write them an email and let them know you will be happy to re-subscribe when they represent people of a variety of sizes, ages, colors and abilities.

***

Defy the fashion police. Wear something you like that you've been told is a "fashion don't" because of your body. Sport horizontal stripes, leggings as pants, pink clothing if you're a readhead, etc. While you rock that look all day, appreciate your body exactly as it looks in these clothes.

***

Do the body love "Hokey Pokey". (This is great to do with kids.) "Put your right arm in, put your right arm out, put your right arm in and love it all around. Do the hokey pokey and joyfully resound, I adore every pound!" Repeat with all body parts. Then put your whole self in and rock out!

***

Go on a media diet. Avoid watching television, looking at billboards or any magazines that exclusively or primarily feature very thin, heavily Photoshopped women. Avoid any publication that lists diets or weight-loss schemes. Notice if how you feel about yourself changes when you're not getting a steady stream of negative messages from those who profit from them.

***

Move 10

Move 10 is the More of Me to Love approach to workplace wellness that encourages people to set aside 10 minutes each day to get away from their desks and move about. This simple approach supports our Health At Every Size® focus and is intended to bring awareness to the lengthy periods we spend sitting down during the day and to remind people that they are welcome to take active breaks.

Move 10 helps people stop thinking about and doing work, stop straining eyes on computer screens and take the opportunity to do something positive for themselves. The movement need not be active exercise, and it's for each person according to that individual's needs and abilities to determine how, and of course if, that movement takes place.

Some people choose to do some light stretching, others walk around the building (either inside or out depending on the weather), and still others just do some refreshing and light calisthenics, amongst other options. Without isolating anyone, we've found that the spirit and fulfillment of Move 10 promotes productivity, creates happiness, fosters camaraderie and enhances focus.

As people have found the joy in this midday respite, many have incorporated more movement into their lives outside of work and increased the amount of time spent on their overall physical and mental well-being.

We're excited to share our Move 10 approach and hope you'll enjoy the simple pleasure that 10 minutes of movement during the day has to offer.

- Jay Solomon

http://www.moreofmetolove.com/

Build yourself a folder (digital or physical) filled with body love heroes and heroines you admire.

***

Watch the movie Hairspray and appreciate the way that Tracy Turnblad and Motormouth Maybelle advocate for themselves and others. Find a way to advocate for yourself.

***

Go outside and go for a walk or roll around the neighborhood. Don't focus on speed or "exercise". Just enjoy moving and seeing the sights. Think about all the journeys your body takes you on every day, and feel the gratitude and connection with your body. Stop whenever it stops feeling fun.

***

Buy a pair of super comfortable slippers. Wear them around and notice how great they make your feet feel.

***

Take a yoga, pilates or Alexander Technique class with a body positive teacher. Focus in engaging with your body in a balanced way.

***

Address a pain point in your body. See if you can determine
the cause, and plan towards resolution.

Pick a part of your body that you're struggling to love. Now touch that body part, caress it, and tell it how much you love it. Apologize to it for all the mean things you've said to it, and promise to only say loving things moving forward. Even if you don't believe it at first, keep doing it.

Get a mammogram, prostrate exam or pap smear. Support your body as it goes through the procedure.

***

Imagine yourself as Godzilla. Now imagine that all your negative body thoughts are down on the floor as part of an imaginary Tokyo. Stomp the stuffing out of your "negative thought" city.

***

Join the "Rolls Not Trolls" Facebook community and help put body positive comments on body negative places on the internet. Message Ragen Chastain on Facebook to be added to the group.

***

Find and listen to a body positive podcast.

***

Take a cooking class and learn to make something you love. Enjoy eating it and appreciate your body's ability to cook and eat this meal.

***

More to Love Mantra — Yes & Yes

A big challenge to overcome when embarking upon greater body acceptance is the very human tendency to make things black and white. Choices around food, health, lifestyle- there are a lot of overlapping concerns, and it's common to put pressure on yourself to come up with the "right way" forward.

To help you find balance and reclaim your innate ability to trust yourself amid new beginnings, I offer this activity called "Yes & Yes".

Out-stretch your left hand and imagine holding within it all the realities of your body, its conditions, limitations, concerns, ailments, worries, fears, beliefs and pains past or present. In this hand, you acknowledge and accept what is real.

Now in your right hand, call to mind feelings of love, of kindness, generosity, patience and hope either given to yourself or to other people. Within this hand, you hold your immense capacity to love and be kind, to be tender and caring- in this hand is your wiser self, the eternal essence of who you are.

Now, join the two hands together in front of your heart - linking both the truths of what you experience with the ability to hold loving wisdom for them. With your hands resting in front of your heart, say aloud these words: "Yes & Yes, I trust in my inner wisdom to guide me because all choices I make empower and support me."

- Rachel Estapa

http://www.moretolovewithrachel.com/

Go somewhere you feel unwelcome and proudly take up space. Realize that people come in all different shapes and sizes, and that everyone deserves to take up the space that they take up.

Read a body positive book.

***

Every time you see your image or reflection (in mirrors, pictures, windows, etc.,) smile and think, "I'm so grateful for my awesome body.

***

Put Post-it notes on your bathroom mirror reminding you how smart, beautiful and talented you are and how awesome your body is.

***

Think of people you admire who have bodies like yours and spend some time reflecting on the similarities between you.

***

Listen for negative body talk and interrupt it. Consider saying something like, "I wish we lived in a world where every body were appreciated."

***

Have a body positive event like a clothing swap where there are specific rules to make it body positive, i.e. no negative body talk, no weight loss talk, etc.

***

Write a list of 10 things you would do if your body were "perfect". Do one of those things. Then choose another.

Treat your body to things that you don't usually take the
time for: massages, soothing showers and lovely lotions. As you
are learning to see your body in a different way, start treating it
in a different way as well.

Fixing Your Relationship with Food

Eating disorder recovery is hard because you never know when the disorder might rear its ugly head, trying to pull you back into its depths. But it's not impossible to fight against a hard day (or a possible relapse) – it just takes conscious thought. And if you've already recognized that you're feeling triggered and that the urges to engage are there, then you're one step toward getting back on track. Now try this:

Breathe. Allow yourself the space to remove yourself from whatever anxiety is causing you to feel triggered. This might take a few breaths; it might take ten minutes of breathing. Give yourself that time.

Relax. Whether that means making a hot cup of tea, slipping into a bubble bath, going for a walk, or meditating, do whatever it is that makes you feel calm. Think: Which activities, people, and places make you feel safe? Seek those out.

Think. Practice intentional thought. Eating disorders steal your rational thought away, twisting reality until you can't recognize it. Take it back. Name the disordered thought. And then tuck it away, replacing it with something rational.

Talk. Rely on your support system – whether that's friends and lovers or medical and mental health professionals. Let them know that you need help, and give them specifics on how to aid you.

Recovery is a journey, and it happens one day – one moment! – at a time. So forgive yourself for any transgressions, and remember that tomorrow is a new day.

- Melissa Fabello

http://www.melissafabello.com/

Declare Your Own Authentic Beauty:

My Beauty Is...

At The Body Positive, we know that experiencing our beauty is not an exercise in vanity, but a way of connecting to the divine nature of our human selves. It is also an excellent way to counteract the voice of fear that wants to attack our bodies for their appearance. Changing our understanding of beauty into something that is non-competitive, all-inclusive, and celebratory is a profound act that leads to deeper self-love and more meaningful connections with others.

On a piece of paper or a page in your journal, write a word or statement to complete the sentences below. Write your answers only, not the statement. Leave space for a few words in front (to the left) of each of your answers.

I feel beautiful when I...
Something about my body I've been teased about is...
I feel self-conscious about my...
I really appreciate my [add body part here] when I am...
I feel radiant when I am...
I love to...
The strangest, quirkiest thing about me is...
I feel unstoppable when I...

Write, "My beauty is" in front of each of your answers to form a complete statement. Don't worry if they are not grammatically correct sentences – you can fix them! Keep your list someplace where you can access it regularly as a reminder that this is your beauty, even parts of you that have been teased or make you feel self-conscious! Do this practice whenever your critic comes to visit.

- Connie Sobczak

http://www.thebodypositive.org/

Every time you see references to bodies being pear-shaped or apple shaped, think (or say out loud) "I'm awesome shaped!"

***

Try a salt scrub. As you scrub your body, think about scrubbing away any negative thoughts you've ever had about it.

***

If there's some part of you that you are having trouble loving, write down three things about that part that you are grateful for.

***

Do something that you used to think was not possible for a person your size.

***

Get a new piercing. Give some special appreciation to the body part you are adorning.

***

Create an online avatar that looks just like you, and be proud to use it.

***

Have a Love Your Body celebration complete with balloons, candles, sparklers and a fancy cake.

***

Be a nude model for artists/art students.

***

Check your posture. See how great it feels in your body to stand up straight.

Do an activity that builds/uses your core strength. Feel the power that radiates from your center.

***

Say a prayer, meditation, or intentional thought of gratitude for your fabulous body.

***

Yell, "I have a good body!" at the top of your lungs, then hug yourself and say, "Thank you body!"

***

Look in the mirror and say something positive out loud to yourself about how fabulous you look.

***

Give your body the day off. Order in food, relax and read. Watch movies or have a Netflix marathon.

***

Remember that people take better care of things that they like than things that they hate. That includes our bodies. Spend some time thinking about how you would treat your body if you loved every single thing about it. Try doing some (or all) of those things right now.

Wear a bathing suit in public. Remember that you aren't just enjoying time at the pool, river, or waterpark. You're also being a role model for others like you why may not yet realize that they are completely worthy of wearing a swimsuit.

***

Realize that size diversity is all around us in nature—from rocks to trees to animals. Bodies come in lots of sizes for lots of reasons. Just like every tree—whether big or small—is a good tree, and every rock—big or small—is a good rock, every body—big or small—is a good body.

***

Take some time protecting your precious body. Test the batteries in the smoke alarms and make sure you have a fire extinguisher near high-risk areas (like the kitchen). Instead of thinking of these jobs as mundane chores, think of them as ways you take good care of yourself.

***

Fill the bathtub with suds and wonderful scents. Settle in for a long soak. Feel your body relax as you thank it for all it does.

***

Pick one small habit that you think would make you feel good and help you honor your body. Commit to doing it at whatever interval feels right for you (daily, 3 times per week, etc.) Celebrate every time you do it.

If loving your body seems too overwhelming, consider trying to get to a place of feeling neutral around your body, or even just liking it a little more than you do right now. Take baby steps.

When you are sick, absolve yourself of guilt and decide to view your situation as you and your body against a problem rather than you against your body. Remember that people of all sizes get sick and that health is never a barometer of worthiness. Think of taking care of your sick body just like you would take care of a sick friend.

***

Get a tattoo that reminds you of your commitment towards loving your body.

***

Drop the utensils and eat something gooey, sticky and wonderful with your fingers. Appreciate your body's ability to enjoy food through so many of your senses.

***

Mirror Confrontation

This is designed to help people confront the reality of their bodies, while reducing self-objectification. You'll look into the mirror and describe your body as precisely and neutrally as possible, while carefully avoiding subjective and negative statements.

Here is an example of a precise and neutral description:

"I have straight blonde hair, brown eyes, and a mole under my right nostril." (all true!)

"Oh, and I also have a rounded belly that sticks out a little bit." (true again.)

Here is an example of a subjective and negative statement:

"I am an ugly unloveable loser." (see the difference?)

Over time, and with repetition, "mirror confrontation" will help you view your body - and the different parts of your body - as neutral facts rather than as subjective signifiers of your moral character and/or entire identity!

- Kjerstin Gruys, Ph.D.

http://www.ayearwithoutmirrors.com/

Get an air matress, find a pool, and spend some time enjoying a good float!

***

Spend more time naked. Dust the house naked. Read books naked. Eat mangos naked. Use the opportunity to really notice and appreciate your body.

***

CHASTAIN, DEPATIE, SCHIAVO-CAMPO

Grab some index cards and write something you love about your body on each card. When you need a pick-me-up, deal yourself a hand of body love.

***

Become an amateur sociologist or people watcher. Go to a public pool and notice how many different kinds of bodies you see. Find something to appreciate about every one.

***

As you drink a glass of water, think about how it helps your body to run well, and marvel at the way that your body uses water in almost every process.

***

When you begin to have a negative thought about your body, become aware of it, and then yell out loud, "That's crap! I am awesome!"

***

Get a pedicure as a present for your awesome feet.

***

Try a new physical activity that helps you build your awesome muscles.

***

Take a mud bath and enjoy the feeling of the mud covering your body.

***

Listen to a body positive speaker live or on YouTube.

***

You and a friend take turns telling each other how amazing you both are.

***

Start a body positive blog, tumblr or Instagram of your own.

***

Introduce someone to the concept of Body Positivity. Invite them to join us.

***

Acknowledge that you live in a culture that perpetuates body hatred—often for a profit. Remember that recognizing that is the first step to opting out. When you find an example, notice it and consciously decide to opt out of it.

***

Spend a day noticing all of the negative messages that you get (especially those that are being used to try to sell you something) and every time you notice, say "That's B.S.!" in your head.

***

Grab a stack of Post-it notes. Take out a photo album and find the pictures of yourself. On each picture of yourself, put a Post-it note saying something positive about you.

***

Conduct a marriage ceremony between you and your body.

***

Make a list of every single thing that you can think of that your body does for you (like breathing, blinking, smiling, hugging, walking or rolling your wheelchair, etc.) Become conscious of your thoughts about your body. Whenever you have a negative thought about your body, replace it with gratitude for something from the list you made in the step above. It doesn't have to be one for one. For example, if you're frustrated with one part of your body, you could replace that with gratitude for another part of your body, for breathing, for biking or your heartbeat.

***

Send an e-mail to a company that doesn't currently accommodate you (whether because of size, dis/ability, or something else) and ask them to do so. Stand up for your body.

***

Lay down some tarp, put up a canvas, strip down, paint up, and run into the canvas to make a one-of-a-kind body print. Hang it somewhere that you can admire it.

***

LOVE IT!

Don't style your hair for a day. Appreciate its unique, natural, just-got-out-of-bed look.

***

Buy a present for your body. Wrap it and write out a card explaining why your body deserves a thank-you present.

***

Find something to complement in every person you see today. Every time you think of a compliment for someone else, compliment yourself.

***

Take your body out on a date. Have dinner, maybe a massage or an inspiring movie.

***

Imagine that your body can hear everything you say about it. Speak kindly, your body is listening.

***

Make a commitment to find something good in everything and everyone today, including yourself.

***

Write a love letter to your body. Write with the kind of passion you would have for a lover or partner. Read it to yourself and be transformed.

***

Go onto an internet forum that discusses what actresses wear and how they look. Post comments that talk only about their work or talent. Remember that we can love our bodies for the way they support our dreams and not just how they look.

***

Sign the Declaration of Body Independence:

http://bit.ly/BodyIndependence

***

Action Item: Smile Whenever You See Your Reflection

Today, whenever you look in a mirror or see your reflection, I want you to smile at yourself. See yourself and smile. You can then do your makeup, or check your outfit, or even if you really must, notice a flaw or two. But at least, at first, I want you to smile.

Smile every time you see yourself even if it's hard. Smile even if you don't want to or it feels false or its really difficult to look at yourself.

Smiling is a wonderfully powerful act. It actually reduces stress and anxiety. It lifts your mood. Imagine if you got a mini-endorphin rush every time you looked in the mirror. Imagine the positive effects it could have on your perception of how you look! I assure you that if you continue to do this very simple act every time you look in the mirror, you will start to feel better and better about yourself and your body.

So that's it for today. Just smile whenever you catch your reflection.

Golda Schein

http://www.bodylovewellness.com/

Write down the body image issue you struggle with the most on a small piece of paper. Then place it face out in a window that gets lots of sun. Come back in a few months, and you'll see that the light has dissolved the words, and with them, their meaning. You are more than body parts. You are amazing!

***

Spend a day wearing no makeup at all or skip shaving your face. Remind yourself you are amazing exactly as you wake up.

***

Create a body love ritual and invite a very close friend or group of friends to share it with you.

***

Have an artist draw, sketch or paint you. See how amazing your body is through somone else's eyes.

***

Find out if you are low on any particular nutrients. If so, eat a food high in that nutrient to nourish your beautiful body.

***

Visit a clothing optional beach or resort. Appreciate the amazing diversity of bodies around you. Appreciate your own body, its beauty unhampered by clothing, as you move through the world.

***

Walk barefoot on grass. Think about your body having roots that go deep into the earth and draw energy from it. Try to feel this connect, even when you're not directly physically connected.

***

Think about how you treat your body. Think about how you treat your friends. If you treat your friends better than you treat your body, do one thing today to start solving that.

***

Get yourself some fancy/sexy/awesome underthings. Wear them under a favorite outfit, for a partner, or just lounging by yourself. As you feel good/sexy/happy in your new underthings, remind yourself that your body is awesome wearing anything or nothing at all.

***

Self-love means accepting that some days are tougher than others. And no one is keeping score. You always get another chance in the next minute, the next hour, or the next day. So if you're having a tough day when it comes to body love, acknowledge that's part of the journey, that you are still on the path, and that everything is ok.

***

Join fitfatties.com. Check out the picture and video galleries as well as the posts. Maybe even post something about yourself.

***

Celebrate National Love Your Body Day (or declare today Love My Body Day.) Feel how you are part of a movement of people who are refusing to take part in the body hate that is so prevalent because it is so profitable.

***

When you find you are having a particularly hard time loving your body, take out a piece of paper and write 10 things you love about your body.

***

LOVE IT!

Get a brand-new haircut. Enjoy!

***

Knit or crochet something soft and warm for your body.

***

Take a deep breath and feel the oxygen nourish every cell.

***

30 days of body love! Commit to trying one technique from this book every single day this month. Make note of each body love technique you use in the following blank chart.

1	2	3	4	5
6	7	8	9	10
11	12	13	14	15
16	17	18	19	20
21	22	23	24	25
26	27	28	29	30

NOTES

NOTES

7 days of body love! Commit to trying one technique from this book every single day this week. Make note of each body love technique you use in the following blank chart.

M o n	T u e	W e d	T h u r	F r i	S a t	S u n

NOTES

NOTES

In Conclusion

Congratulations on getting here! Wondering what to do next?

You can start back at the beginning – we are bombarded with negative messages about our bodies so our body love journey isn't something we complete, it's always a path that we are on. Each time you do (and re-do) these exercises you affirm what you know about your amazing body, and you give yourself a chance to dig deeper.

You can check out the Body Love Obstacle Course. This is a proven, step-by-step program that will give you the tools, coaching, and community to create a rock-solid foundation of self-esteem and body love, and teach you the strategies and skills you'll need to leverage that to create the life you've always wanted no matter what obstacles the world puts in your way. We offer live classes as well as a self-paced e-course.

You can check out our guest coaches (the links are included with their exercises throughout this book) who often offer amazing programs that can help you on your journey.

We wish you the very best on your journey of appreciating and loving your amazing body and we look forward to seeing you again on the journey!

About the Authors

Ragen Chastain is a Certified Health Coach, three-time National Champion dancer and marathoner who writes and speaks full-time about self-esteem, body image, and health. Ragen is the author of the blog DancesWithFat, the book Fat: The Owner's Manual, editor of the anthology "The Politics of Size," and serves on the Editorial Board for *Fat Studies: An Interdisciplinary Journal of Body Weight and Society.* Her writing has been published internationally and she has been a guest on news programs on every major network in the US, and many across the globe.

Ragen is a feature interviewee in the documentaries "America the Beautiful 2 – The Thin Commandments" (Warner Brothers,) "A Stage for Size" (USC Films,) "Ragen's More Cabaret" (PBS Independent Lens.) Ragen is the co-founder of the Fit Fatties Forum, and in her free time she is training for her second marathon and her first IRONMAN triathlon.

Jeanette DePatie is a plus-sized, certified fitness instructor, best-selling author and professional speaker who has helped thousands of people of all shapes, sizes, ages and abilities who haven't exercised in a while (or ever) to learn to love their bodies and love exercise again. Via her best-selling book and DVD *The Fat Chick Works Out!* as well as her website everybodycanexercise.com Jeanette offers practical exercise for exercise afficianados as well as klutzes, wimps and absolute beginners.

Jeanette is also an entrepreneur and techsplainer who raised her first million dollars in venture capital before even finishing college. Jeanette has been featured on or in the Katie Couric Show, Dr. Drew, NPR, CBS Interactive, Fox, Livestrong.com, ABC, *The New York Times*, Al Jazeera, *The Wall St. Journal, Women's Running* and *Psychology Today*. You can learn more about her at propellerhead-inc.com/jeanettedepatie.

Pia Schiavo-Campo is a feminist writer, speaker, and social justice activist who is committed to facilitating transformation for marginalized people through coaching and improvisation. She is also the author of the blog Chronicles of a Mixed Fat Chick, which tackles the intersections of race, class, gender, and size. Her agenda includes extinguishing conventional notions of beauty and enoughness by empowering women to take up as much space as they please. Her passion for changing the representation of women of size and women of color in the media is a challenge she embraces daily. She is also a proud partner of the Yoga and Body Coalition, whose mission is to work with all of the ways yoga and body image intersect to create access and dignity for all.

Pia has written many articles on the subject of body image and radical self-acceptance. She believes that when we allow others to stand in their power, anything is possible. She is inspired by the strong women in her life, especially her mother, Hazel, who was her first feminist role model. Pia is Black and Sicilian, speaks Italian fluently, and lives in Los Angeles her awesome husband, Will.

Toni Tails is a full-time artist (http://tonitails.com) and single, home schooling mom of an awesome Autistic kid. She uses her art to promote the beauty of all kinds of bodies, including fat ladies such as herself. She loves spending time with her family, belting out some mean karaoke, reading, and being as silly as humanly possible. (Maybe more!) She has a degree in Nerdism , is a raving Whovian, and often makes poor attempts at quoting films and T.V. shows at inopportune moments.

L O V E   I T !

Thanks for reading! Please add a short review on Amazon and let us know what you thought!

Thanks for reading, we hope that you enjoyed this book as much as we enjoyed creating it! Here are some next steps:

Leave a review on Amazon

Send a testimonial to Jeanette@thefatchick.com

Get $20 off the Body Love Obstacle Course! Go to:

http://realbigpublishing.com/product/body-love-obstacle-course-power-circle-edition/

and use the coupon code: LOVEit20 to get $20 off the regular price.

Get a copy of this book for a friend! Go to:

http://realbigpublishing.com/product/loveit/

and use the coupon code LOVEitFriend15 to receive 15% off the book price.

To see more resources, check out
http://realbigpublishing.com/product-category/ragen-chastain/

Thanks and good luck!
Jeanette, Pia, Ragen and Toni